Personal Information

Name:	Date of Birth:
Adress:	
Business Adress:	
Email:	
Mobile Telephone:	
Home Telephone:	
Fax:	

Emergency Contact

Name:	Relationship:
Adress:	
Mobile Telephone:	
Home Telephone:	
Email:	

Notes

Vehicle Information

Vehicle:	Year:
Make:	
Model:	
Engine:	
VIN Number:	
Purchase Date:	Mileage at Purchase:
Purchase Form:	

Insurance Company

Company Name:	
Adress:	
Office:	Work:
Phone:	Fax:
Email:	
Website:	
Agent:	Phone:
Cost:	
Insurance Numbre:	
Cover Details:	
Start Date:	End Date:

Notes

YEAR: _____ MONTH: _____ MODEL: _____

Date / Time	Oil Changed	Air Filter	Balance Tires	Wheel Alignment	Fuel Filter	Brakes Serviced	Spark Plugs	Transmission	Wiper Blades	Batteries	Radiator	Belts&Hoses	Mileage

make: _____   date purchased: _____

model: _____   purchased price: _____

license plate: _____   purchased form: _____

DATE/TIME	MAINTENANCE/COMMENTS	MILEAGE

Date / Time	Oil Changed	Air Filter	Balance Tires	Wheel Alignment	Fuel Filter	Brakes Serviced	Spark Plugs	Transmission	Wiper Blades	Batteries	Radiator	Belts&Hoses	Mileage

YEAR: _____   MONTH: _____   MODEL: _____

make: _____   date purchased: _____

model: _____   purchased price: _____

license plate: _____   purchased form: _____

DATE/TIME	MAINTENANCE/COMMENTS	MILEAGE

Date / Time	Oil Changed	Air Filter	Balance Tires	Wheel Alignment	Fuel Filter	Brakes Serviced	Spark Plugs	Transmission	Wiper Blades	Batteries	Radiator	Belts&Hoses	Mileage

YEAR: _____ MONTH: _____ MODEL: _____

| make: | date purchased: |

| model: | purchased price: |

| license plate: | purchased form: |

Date/Time	Maintenance/Comments	Mileage

Date/Time	Oil Changed	Air Filter	Balance Tires	Wheel Alignment	Fuel Filter	Brakes Serviced	Spark Plugs	Transmission	Wiper Blades	Batteries	Radiator	Belts&Hoses	Mileage

YEAR: _____ MONTH: _____ MODEL: _____

make: _____

model: _____

license plate: _____

date purchased: _____

purchased price: _____

purchased form: _____

Date/Time	Maintenance/Comments	Mileage

Date/Time	Oil Changed	Air Filter	Balance Tires	Wheel Alignment	Fuel Filter	Brakes Serviced	Spark Plugs	Transmission	Wiper Blades	Batteries	Radiator	Belts&Hoses	Mileage

YEAR: _____ MONTH: _____ MODEL: _____

make:		date purchased:	
model:		purchased price:	
license plate:		purchased form:	

DATE/TIME	MAINTENANCE/COMMENTS	MILEAGE

YEAR: _____ **MONTH:** _____ **MODEL:** _____

Date / Time	Oil Changed	Air Filter	Balance Tires	Wheel Alignment	Fuel Filter	Brakes Serviced	Spark Plugs	Transmission	Wiper Blades	Batteries	Radiator	Belts&Hoses	Mileage

make:	date purchased:
model:	purchased price:
license plate:	purchased form:

DATE/TIME	MAINTENANCE/COMMENTS	MILEAGE

Date / Time	Oil Changed	Air Filter	Balance Tires	Wheel Alignment	Fuel Filter	Brakes Serviced	Spark Plugs	Transmission	Wiper Blades	Batteries	Radiator	Belts&Hoses	Mileage

make: _____   date purchased: _____

model: _____   purchased price: _____

license plate: _____   purchased form: _____

Date/Time	Maintenance/Comments	Mileage

Date / Time	Oil Changed	Air Filter	Balance Tires	Wheel Alignment	Fuel Filter	Brakes Serviced	Spark Plugs	Transmission	Wiper Blades	Batteries	Radiator	Belts&Hoses	Mileage

YEAR: _____ MONTH: _____ MODEL: _____

make: _____ date purchased: _____

model: _____ purchased price: _____

license plate: _____ purchased form: _____

Date/Time	Maintenance/Comments	Mileage

YEAR: _____ MONTH: _____ MODEL: _____

Date / Time	Oil Changed	Air Filter	Balance Tires	Wheel Alignment	Fuel Filter	Brakes Serviced	Spark Plugs	Transmission	Wiper Blades	Batteries	Radiator	Belts&Hoses	Mileage

make: _____   date purchased: _____

model: _____   purchased price: _____

license plate: _____   purchased form: _____

DATE/TIME	MAINTENANCE/COMMENTS	MILEAGE

YEAR: _____ MONTH: _____ MODEL: _____

Date / Time	Oil Changed	Air Filter	Balance Tires	Wheel Alignment	Fuel Filter	Brakes Serviced	Spark Plugs	Transmission	Wiper Blades	Batteries	Radiator	Belts&Hoses	Mileage

make:			date purchased:

model:	purchased price:

license plate:	purchased form:

Date/Time	Maintenance/Comments	Mileage

Date / Time	Oil Changed	Air Filter	Balance Tires	Wheel Alignment	Fuel Filter	Brakes Serviced	Spark Plugs	Transmission	Wiper Blades	Batteries	Radiator	Belts&Hoses	Mileage

YEAR: _____ MONTH: _____ MODEL: _____

make: _____   date purchased: _____

model: _____   purchased price: _____

license plate: _____   purchased form: _____

DATE/TIME	MAINTENANCE/COMMENTS	MILEAGE

YEAR: _____ MONTH: _____ MODEL: _____

Date / Time	Oil Changed	Air Filter	Balance Tires	Wheel Alignment	Fuel Filter	Brakes Serviced	Spark Plugs	Transmission	Wiper Blades	Batteries	Radiator	Belts&Hoses	Mileage

make:	date purchased:
model:	purchased price:
license plate:	purchased form:

Date/Time	Maintenance/Comments	Mileage

YEAR:	MONTH:											MODEL:

Date / Time	Oil Changed	Air Filter	Balance Tires	Wheel Alignment	Fuel Filter	Brakes Serviced	Spark Plugs	Transmission	Wiper Blades	Batteries	Radiator	Belts&Hoses	Mileage

make: _____   date purchased: _____

model: _____   purchased price: _____

license plate: _____   purchased form: _____

DATE/TIME	MAINTENANCE/COMMENTS	MILEAGE

YEAR: _____ MONTH: _____ MODEL: _____

Date / Time	Oil Changed	Air Filter	Balance Tires	Wheel Alignment	Fuel Filter	Brakes Serviced	Spark Plugs	Transmission	Wiper Blades	Batteries	Radiator	Belts&Hoses	Mileage

make: _____   date purchased: _____

model: _____   purchased price: _____

license plate: _____   purchased form: _____

Date/Time	Maintenance/Comments	Mileage

YEAR: _____ MONTH: _____ MODEL: _____

Date / Time	Oil Changed	Air Filter	Balance Tires	Wheel Alignment	Fuel Filter	Brakes Serviced	Spark Plugs	Transmission	Wiper Blades	Batteries	Radiator	Belts&Hoses	Mileage

make: _____   date purchased: _____

model: _____   purchased price: _____

license plate: _____   purchased form: _____

Date/Time	Maintenance/Comments	Mileage

Date / Time	Oil Changed	Air Filter	Balance Tires	Wheel Alignment	Fuel Filter	Brakes Serviced	Spark Plugs	Transmission	Wiper Blades	Batteries	Radiator	Belts&Hoses	Mileage

YEAR: _____ MONTH: _____ MODEL: _____

make: _____   date purchased: _____

model: _____   purchased price: _____

license plate: _____   purchased form: _____

DATE/TIME	MAINTENANCE/COMMENTS	MILEAGE

Date/Time	Oil Changed	Air Filter	Balance Tires	Wheel Alignment	Fuel Filter	Brakes Serviced	Spark Plugs	Transmission	Wiper Blades	Batteries	Radiator	Belts&Hoses	Mileage

YEAR: _____ MONTH: _____ MODEL: _____

make: _____   date purchased: _____

model: _____   purchased price: _____

license plate: _____   purchased form: _____

Date/Time	Maintenance/Comments	Mileage

YEAR: _____ MONTH: _____ MODEL: _____

Date/Time	Oil Changed	Air Filter	Balance Tires	Wheel Alignment	Fuel Filter	Brakes Serviced	Spark Plugs	Transmission	Wiper Blades	Batteries	Radiator	Belts&Hoses	Mileage

make: _____   date purchased: _____

model: _____   purchased price: _____

license plate: _____   purchased form: _____

DATE/TIME	MAINTENANCE/COMMENTS	MILEAGE

Date / Time	Oil Changed	Air Filter	Balance Tires	Wheel Alignment	Fuel Filter	Brakes Serviced	Spark Plugs	Transmission	Wiper Blades	Batteries	Radiator	Belts&Hoses	Mileage

make: _____   date purchased: _____

model: _____   purchased price: _____

license plate: _____   purchased form: _____

DATE/TIME	MAINTENANCE/COMMENTS	MILEAGE

YEAR: _____ MONTH: _____ MODEL: _____

Date / Time	Oil Changed	Air Filter	Balance Tires	Wheel Alignment	Fuel Filter	Brakes Serviced	Spark Plugs	Transmission	Wiper Blades	Batteries	Radiator	Belts&Hoses	Mileage

make: _____   date purchased: _____

model: _____   purchased price: _____

license plate: _____   purchased form: _____

Date/Time	Maintenance/Comments	Mileage

YEAR: _____ MONTH: _____ MODEL: _____

Date / Time	Oil Changed	Air Filter	Balance Tires	Wheel Alignment	Fuel Filter	Brakes Serviced	Spark Plugs	Transmission	Wiper Blades	Batteries	Radiator	Belts&Hoses	Mileage

make: _____   date purchased: _____

model: _____   purchased price: _____

license plate: _____   purchased form: _____

Date/Time	Maintenance/Comments	Mileage

YEAR: _____ MONTH: _____ MODEL: _____

Date / Time	Oil Changed	Air Filter	Balance Tires	Wheel Alignment	Fuel Filter	Brakes Serviced	Spark Plugs	Transmission	Wiper Blades	Batteries	Radiator	Belts&Hoses	Mileage

make: _____   date purchased: _____

model: _____   purchased price: _____

license plate: _____   purchased form: _____

Date/Time	Maintenance/Comments	Mileage

Date / Time	Oil Changed	Air Filter	Balance Tires	Wheel Alignment	Fuel Filter	Brakes Serviced	Spark Plugs	Transmission	Wiper Blades	Batteries	Radiator	Belts&Hoses	Mileage

YEAR: _____ MONTH: _____ MODEL: _____

make: _____ date purchased: _____

model: _____ purchased price: _____

license plate: _____ purchased form: _____

Date/Time	Maintenance/Comments	Mileage

YEAR: _____ MONTH: _____ MODEL: _____

Date / Time	Oil Changed	Air Filter	Balance Tires	Wheel Alignment	Fuel Filter	Brakes Serviced	Spark Plugs	Transmission	Wiper Blades	Batteries	Radiator	Belts&Hoses	Mileage

make: _____   date purchased: _____

model: _____   purchased price: _____

license plate: _____   purchased form: _____

Date/Time	Maintenance/Comments	Mileage

YEAR: _____ MONTH: _____ MODEL: _____

Date / Time	Oil Changed	Air Filter	Balance Tires	Wheel Alignment	Fuel Filter	Brakes Serviced	Spark Plugs	Transmission	Wiper Blades	Batteries	Radiator	Belts&Hoses	Mileage

make: _____   date purchased: _____

model: _____   purchased price: _____

license plate: _____   purchased form: _____

DATE/TIME	MAINTENANCE/COMMENTS	MILEAGE

YEAR: _____ MONTH: _____ MODEL: _____

Date / Time	Oil Changed	Air Filter	Balance Tires	Wheel Alignment	Fuel Filter	Brakes Serviced	Spark Plugs	Transmission	Wiper Blades	Batteries	Radiator	Belts&Hoses	Mileage

make: _____   date purchased: _____

model: _____   purchased price: _____

license plate: _____   purchased form: _____

Date/Time	Maintenance/Comments	Mileage

YEAR: _____ MONTH: _____ MODEL: _____

Date / Time	Oil Changed	Air Filter	Balance Tires	Wheel Alignment	Fuel Filter	Brakes Serviced	Spark Plugs	Transmission	Wiper Blades	Batteries	Radiator	Belts&Hoses	Mileage

make:	date purchased:
model:	purchased price:
license plate:	purchased form:

DATE/TIME	MAINTENANCE/COMMENTS	MILEAGE

Date / Time	Oil Changed	Air Filter	Balance Tires	Wheel Alignment	Fuel Filter	Brakes Serviced	Spark Plugs	Transmission	Wiper Blades	Batteries	Radiator	Belts&Hoses	Mileage

YEAR: _____ MONTH: _____ MODEL: _____

make: _____   date purchased: _____

model: _____   purchased price: _____

license plate: _____   purchased form: _____

DATE/TIME	MAINTENANCE/COMMENTS	MILEAGE

Date / Time	Oil Changed	Air Filter	Balance Tires	Wheel Alignment	Fuel Filter	Brakes Serviced	Spark Plugs	Transmission	Wiper Blades	Batteries	Radiator	Belts&Hoses	Mileage

YEAR: _____   MONTH: _____   MODEL: _____

make: _____   date purchased: _____

model: _____   purchased price: _____

license plate: _____   purchased form: _____

DATE/TIME	MAINTENANCE/COMMENTS	MILEAGE

YEAR: _____ MONTH: _____ MODEL: _____

Date / Time	Oil Changed	Air Filter	Balance Tires	Wheel Alignment	Fuel Filter	Brakes Serviced	Spark Plugs	Transmission	Wiper Blades	Batteries	Radiator	Belts&Hoses	Mileage

make: _____   date purchased: _____

model: _____   purchased price: _____

license plate: _____   purchased form: _____

DATE/TIME	MAINTENANCE/COMMENTS	MILEAGE

YEAR: _____ MONTH: _____ MODEL: _____

Date/Time	Oil Changed	Air Filter	Balance Tires	Wheel Alignment	Fuel Filter	Brakes Serviced	Spark Plugs	Transmission	Wiper Blades	Batteries	Radiator	Belts&Hoses	Mileage

make: _____

model: _____

license plate: _____

date purchased: _____

purchased price: _____

purchased form: _____

DATE/TIME	MAINTENANCE/COMMENTS	MILEAGE

YEAR: _____ MONTH: _____ MODEL: _____

Date / Time	Oil Changed	Air Filter	Balance Tires	Wheel Alignment	Fuel Filter	Brakes Serviced	Spark Plugs	Transmission	Wiper Blades	Batteries	Radiator	Belts&Hoses	Mileage

make: _____ date purchased: _____

model: _____ purchased price: _____

license plate: _____ purchased form: _____

DATE/TIME	MAINTENANCE/COMMENTS	MILEAGE

YEAR: _____ MONTH: _____ MODEL: _____

Date / Time	Oil Changed	Air Filter	Balance Tires	Wheel Alignment	Fuel Filter	Brakes Serviced	Spark Plugs	Transmission	Wiper Blades	Batteries	Radiator	Belts&Hoses	Mileage

make:		date purchased:
model:		purchased price:
license plate:		purchased form:

DATE/TIME	MAINTENANCE/COMMENTS	MILEAGE

YEAR: _____ MONTH: _____ MODEL: _____

Date/Time	Oil Changed	Air Filter	Balance Tires	Wheel Alignment	Fuel Filter	Brakes Serviced	Spark Plugs	Transmission	Wiper Blades	Batteries	Radiator	Belts&Hoses	Mileage

make: _____   date purchased: _____

model: _____   purchased price: _____

license plate: _____   purchased form: _____

Date/Time	Maintenance/Comments	Mileage

YEAR: _____ MONTH: _____ MODEL: _____

Date / Time	Oil Changed	Air Filter	Balance Tires	Wheel Alignment	Fuel Filter	Brakes Serviced	Spark Plugs	Transmission	Wiper Blades	Batteries	Radiator	Belts&Hoses	Mileage

make: _____ date purchased: _____

model: _____ purchased price: _____

license plate: _____ purchased form: _____

Date/Time	Maintenance/Comments	Mileage

Date / Time	Oil Changed	Air Filter	Balance Tires	Wheel Alignment	Fuel Filter	Brakes Serviced	Spark Plugs	Transmission	Wiper Blades	Batteries	Radiator	Belts&Hoses	Mileage

YEAR: _____ MONTH: _____ MODEL: _____

make:		date purchased:
model:		purchased price:
license plate:		purchased form:

Date/Time	Maintenance/Comments	Mileage

YEAR: _____ **MONTH:** _____ **MODEL:** _____

Date / Time	Oil Changed	Air Filter	Balance Tires	Wheel Alignment	Fuel Filter	Brakes Serviced	Spark Plugs	Transmission	Wiper Blades	Batteries	Radiator	Belts&Hoses	Mileage

make: _____ date purchased: _____

model: _____ purchased price: _____

license plate: _____ purchased form: _____

Date/Time	Maintenance/Comments	Mileage

YEAR: _____ MONTH: _____ MODEL: _____

Date / Time	Oil Changed	Air Filter	Balance Tires	Wheel Alignment	Fuel Filter	Brakes Serviced	Spark Plugs	Transmission	Wiper Blades	Batteries	Radiator	Belts&Hoses	Mileage

make: _____   date purchased: _____

model: _____   purchased price: _____

license plate: _____   purchased form: _____

DATE/TIME	MAINTENANCE/COMMENTS	MILEAGE

YEAR: _____ MONTH: _____ MODEL: _____

Date / Time	Oil Changed	Air Filter	Balance Tires	Wheel Alignment	Fuel Filter	Brakes Serviced	Spark Plugs	Transmission	Wiper Blades	Batteries	Radiator	Belts&Hoses	Mileage

make: _____   date purchased: _____

model: _____   purchased price: _____

license plate: _____   purchased form: _____

DATE/TIME	MAINTENANCE/COMMENTS	MILEAGE

YEAR: _____ MONTH: _____ MODEL: _____

Date / Time	Oil Changed	Air Filter	Balance Tires	Wheel Alignment	Fuel Filter	Brakes Serviced	Spark Plugs	Transmission	Wiper Blades	Batteries	Radiator	Belts&Hoses	Mileage

make: _____   date purchased: _____

model: _____   purchased price: _____

license plate: _____   purchased form: _____

Date/Time	Maintenance/Comments	Mileage

YEAR: _____ **MONTH:** _____ **MODEL:** _____

Date / Time	Oil Changed	Air Filter	Balance Tires	Wheel Alignment	Fuel Filter	Brakes Serviced	Spark Plugs	Transmission	Wiper Blades	Batteries	Radiator	Belts&Hoses	Mileage

make: _____   date purchased: _____

model: _____   purchased price: _____

license plate: _____   purchased form: _____

DATE/TIME	MAINTENANCE/COMMENTS	MILEAGE

YEAR: _____ **MONTH:** _____ **MODEL:** _____

Date / Time	Oil Changed	Air Filter	Balance Tires	Wheel Alignment	Fuel Filter	Brakes Serviced	Spark Plugs	Transmission	Wiper Blades	Batteries	Radiator	Belts&Hoses	Mileage

make: _____   date purchased: _____

model: _____   purchased price: _____

license plate: _____   purchased form: _____

Date/Time	Maintenance/Comments	Mileage

YEAR: _____ MONTH: _____ MODEL: _____

Date / Time	Oil Changed	Air Filter	Balance Tires	Wheel Alignment	Fuel Filter	Brakes Serviced	Spark Plugs	Transmission	Wiper Blades	Batteries	Radiator	Belts&Hoses	Mileage

make: _____   date purchased: _____

model: _____   purchased price: _____

license plate: _____   purchased form: _____

DATE/TIME	MAINTENANCE/COMMENTS	MILEAGE

YEAR: _____ MONTH: _____ MODEL: _____

Date / Time	Oil Changed	Air Filter	Balance Tires	Wheel Alignment	Fuel Filter	Brakes Serviced	Spark Plugs	Transmission	Wiper Blades	Batteries	Radiator	Belts&Hoses	Mileage

make: _____   date purchased: _____

model: _____   purchased price: _____

license plate: _____   purchased form: _____

DATE/TIME	MAINTENANCE/COMMENTS	MILEAGE

YEAR: _____ MONTH: _____ MODEL: _____

Date / Time	Oil Changed	Air Filter	Balance Tires	Wheel Alignment	Fuel Filter	Brakes Serviced	Spark Plugs	Transmission	Wiper Blades	Batteries	Radiator	Belts&Hoses	Mileage

make: _____   date purchased: _____

model: _____   purchased price: _____

license plate: _____   purchased form: _____

Date/Time	Maintenance/Comments	Mileage

YEAR: _____ **MONTH:** _____ **MODEL:** _____

Date/Time	Oil Changed	Air Filter	Balance Tires	Wheel Alignment	Fuel Filter	Brakes Serviced	Spark Plugs	Transmission	Wiper Blades	Batteries	Radiator	Belts&Hoses	Mileage

make: _____   date purchased: _____

model: _____   purchased price: _____

license plate: _____   purchased form: _____

Date/Time	Maintenance/Comments	Mileage

YEAR: _____ MONTH: _____ MODEL: _____

Date / Time	Oil Changed	Air Filter	Balance Tires	Wheel Alignment	Fuel Filter	Brakes Serviced	Spark Plugs	Transmission	Wiper Blades	Batteries	Radiator	Belts&Hoses	Mileage

YEARLY SUMMARY

month	total distance	total cost of fuel	total repairs	total maint.
jan				
feb				
mar				
apr				
may				
jun				
jul				
aug				
sep				
oct				
nov				
dec				

Thank you!

WE ARE GLAD THAT YOU PURCHASED OUR
BOOK!
PLEASE LET US KNOW HOW WE CAN IMPROVE IT!
YOUR FEEDBACK IS ESSENTIAL TO US.

Contact us at:

M log'Sin@gmail.com

JUST TITLE THE EMAIL 'CREATIVE' AND WE WILL

GIVE YOU SOME EXTRA SURPRISES!

www.ingramcontent.com/pod-product-compliance
Lightning Source LLC
Chambersburg PA
CBHW071458210326
41597CB00018B/2593